UNUSUAL PETS

First published in Great Britain in 2019
by Hodder and Stoughton Limited

Copyright © Hodder and Stoughton, 2019

Editor: Victoria Brooker
Produced for Wayland by Dynamo
Written by Pat Jacobs

MIX
Paper from
responsible sources
FSC® C104740

FSC
www.fsc.org

HBK ISBN: 978 1 5263 1007 1
PBK ISBN: 978 1 5263 1008 8

10 9 8 7 6 5 4 3 2 1

Wayland, an imprint of
Hachette Children's Group
Part of Hodder and Stoughton
Carmelite House
50 Victoria Embankment
London EC4Y 0DZ

An Hachette UK Company
www.hachette.co.uk
www.hachettechildrens.co.uk

Printed and bound in China

Picture acknowledgements:

All images courtesy of Getty Images iStock apart from: p7 tr Shutterstock, p23 c Shutterstock

(Key: tr-top right, c-centre)

CONTENTS

Unusual pets   4

Chinchillas   6

Degus   8

Snakes   10

Terrapins   12

Salamanders   14

Axolotls   16

Newts   18

Frogs   20

Madagascar hissing cockroaches   22

Stick insects and mantises   24

Giant land snails   26

Quiz   28

Quiz answers   30

Glossary   31

Index   32

UNUSUAL PETS

If you're looking for a pet pal with a difference, check out these cool creatures.

CHAMPION CHEWERS

Chinchillas and degus are South American rodents. These active animals need large, tall cages with plenty of space to jump and climb. Rodents' teeth never stop growing, so they have to chew to wear them down. Give these pets lots of chewing material in their cages, otherwise they may gnaw on the furniture when you let them out.

REMARKABLE REPTILES

Reptiles such as snakes and terrapins are cold-blooded creatures, so they need to bask under a heat lamp to raise their body temperature. They also need an ultraviolet light to keep them healthy. Reptiles carry salmonella, so it's very important to wash your hands after handling them.

AWESOME AMPHIBIANS

Amphibians start life in water, then grow legs and lungs. As adults, some live on land and others spend all or part of their time in water, but they all need damp conditions and dark hiding places. Amphibians have sensitive, delicate skin and should be handled as little as possible. Members of the salamander family, including axolotls and newts, can regrow lost limbs.

INTRIGUING INVERTEBRATES

Insects and snails are invertebrates. Their bodies are protected by a tough outer shell that allows them to live in places where other creatures wouldn't survive. An insect's shell is called an exoskeleton and, because it doesn't grow, insects have to shed it as they get bigger. Shedding, or moulting, is a dangerous time in an insect's life as their new exoskeleton is very delicate until it hardens.

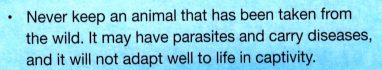

TOP TIPS

- Never keep an animal that has been taken from the wild. It may have parasites and carry diseases, and it will not adapt well to life in captivity.

- Some of these animals have surprisingly long lifespans, so think about whether you'll be able to look after your pet for the rest of its natural life.

- Don't allow your pets to breed unless you have homes for the babies – keep them in single-sex pairs or groups, or destroy any eggs.

- Never release an unwanted pet into the wild. Captive animals rarely have the skills to survive and you could upset the balance of the natural environment.

- Consider getting a pet from a rehoming centre. Buying an older animal is a good solution if you're not sure you can care for it for 20-30 years.

CHINCHILLAS

Chinchillas are nocturnal animals so they sleep during the day. They are active in the early mornings and evenings and need to be let out of their cage at least once a day. They can live for more than 15 years.

TWO IS COMPANY

A single chinchilla will be lonely, so it will need at least one pal. It's best to choose same-sex littermates, or a neutered male and a female. If chinchillas don't already know each other, keep them side by side in separate cages until they get used to one another's scent. When you move them into the same cage, put their beds at opposite ends and give them separate dust baths until they're firm friends.

ROOM TO CLIMB

Chinchillas need a large cage with platforms to jump onto and branches to climb. They have very thick fur and can survive cold temperatures but draughts are dangerous, so keep them indoors. The cage should be away from radiators and out of direct sunlight because they can easily overheat – if your pet's ears go red it's too hot. Chinchillas need a hay-filled nest box that's big enough for them to cuddle up together, with an extra box so they can sleep alone if they want their own space.

TAMING AND EXERCISE

Before you let your chinchilla out of its cage you'll need to tame it so you can catch it again. Raisins are a favourite treat, so train your pet to come to you for a raisin and gently stroke it under the chin. Early evening is a good time to let your chinchilla out. Keep it confined to a small space and watch it carefully. Chinchillas love to explore and will chew anything – including electric cables.

KEEPING CLEAN

Chinchillas clean their fur by bathing in fine dust, so you'll need a dust bath for your pet. You can buy chinchilla dust from pet stores and it should be changed about once a week. Never use sand because it's too coarse and never put water on your chinchilla. If it gets wet, dry it with a towel immediately.

FEEDING

Chinchillas need vitamin C so chinchilla pellets are the best food for them. Good quality hay provides fibre and wears down their teeth, too. Don't give them too many treats – a rich diet can make chinchillas ill. They should always have fresh drinking water.

UNDERSTAND YOUR PET

I love to play with cardboard boxes, so put one or two in my cage. I'll probably chew them up so make sure you take away any staples or plastic tape.

DEGUS

Degus make cute pets. They're active during the day, rarely bite and love busy homes with lots of attention from their owners. They are social animals and should be kept in pairs or groups. They live for five to nine years.

UNDERSTAND YOUR PET

Scoop me up from underneath my body. If you grab me from above, I'll think you're a bird of prey.

Degus need a sand bath at least twice a week to keep their fur clean.

FEEDING

You can buy pellets for degus that provide everything they need to stay healthy. Sugar is very bad for them and they can easily get diabetes, so don't feed your pets fruit or sweet vegetables such as corn. They'll enjoy some leafy greens and should always have some good quality hay in their cage to nibble on.

DEGU BEHAVIOUR

Degus are social animals and communicate using noises such as tweets, chirps, whistles and grunts. They come from Chile where they work together to build complicated burrows with nesting areas and food stores. Degus have ultraviolet vision – the white markings on their chest reflect ultraviolet light and show up when they stand on their hind legs to give an alarm signal.

HOME COMFORTS

These active animals need big cages with plenty of exercise space and different levels and ramps. If the cage has a wire mesh floor, cover it with cardboard or hemp matting because it will damage your pets' feet. Degus love to dig and burrow, so they'll enjoy a box filled with potting compost or sand and some clay pipe tunnels. They can easily overheat so they should be kept at a temperature below 20°C (68°F), and they hate wet or damp conditions.

CLEVER CREATURES

Degus are inquisitive and intelligent – scientists have taught them how to use a rake to get food and they can be trained to use a litter box. Tree branches such as apple, pear, oak, beech or ash, will keep your pets busy and give them something to gnaw on, and they enjoy a treat ball or exercise wheel.

GOOD TO KNOW

Degus have orange teeth and if their teeth turn white it's a sign that they're not well. You should never catch your degu by its tail because it can shed the skin and run away. This is how they escape from predators.

SNAKES

Snakes are fascinating creatures and they can become tame pets. Many live for more than 20 years, so keeping a snake is a long-term commitment – and you'll need someone who's willing to look after your slithery pal if you go away.

SETTING UP A VIVARIUM

Snakes need an escape-proof tank long enough for them to stretch out fully. The width and height should be at least one third of their length. Reptiles need a heat lamp over one side of the tank – the warm side should be 28-30°C (82.5-86°F) and the cool side 20-24 °C (68-75°F), and they need an ultraviolet light. Although snakes don't drink water, you should provide a shallow bowlful to keep the air moist and in case your pet wants to soak in it.

FEEDING YOUR SNAKE

Snakes eat small animals, so you must be prepared to handle frozen baby mice, rats or chicks. Never feed your snake live rodents because they might bite your pet. Make sure that a snake will accept dead prey before you buy it because some will only take live food. Snakes can open their jaws very wide and they swallow their prey whole. They normally only need to eat once a week, or once every two weeks.

UNDERSTAND YOUR PET

Please make sure my food is completely defrosted and it's no wider than one and a half times the width of my body.

SKIN SHEDDING

Snakes shed their skins regularly. If your pet hides, stops eating, its skin looks dull and its eyes look cloudy, it may be about to shed. This is a stressful time for a snake. You can help by making sure it has a shallow dish of clean water to soak in and put some smooth rocks or driftwood in the enclosure for your pet to rub against.

BEST SNAKES FOR BEGINNERS

- Garter snakes: Garter snakes are alert and active during the day. Females are about 90 cm (3ft) long, while males are smaller. They live for up to 10 years.

- Corn snakes: Corn snakes are constrictors and kill their prey by squeezing it until it suffocates. They can grow up to 180 cm (6 ft) long and live for up to 20 years or more.

- Milk snakes: These slow-moving constrictors grow up to 150 cm (5 ft) long and live for up to 12 years. They are nocturnal and should always be housed alone because one snake may eat the other.

- Ball pythons: Ball pythons, also called royal pythons, grow up to 150 cm (5 ft) long and can live for up to 30, and even 50, years. They can be picky eaters, so make sure yours will eat dead prey before you take it home.

TERRAPINS

Terrapins, sometimes called turtles, make great family pets, but they need a lot of space and care. Some terrapins live for up to 30 years and larger species may have to be moved to outdoor ponds when they are fully grown.

FEEDING

Offer your pets a variety of foods including raw meat and fish, snails, live insects and worms, berries and leafy vegetables. Terrapin pellets are also available. Terrapins eat in the water and uneaten food drops to the bottom. This makes the water dirty, so many owners feed their pets in a separate water tank or bowl that's easy to clean.

TERRAPIN TANKS

Terrapins need warm water to swim in and a dry area where they can bask under a heat lamp. Allow 80 litres (20 gal) of water per 5 cm (2 in) of shell length based on the adult size of your pets. They should be able to swim without breaking the surface or touching the sides or bottom of the tank. Dirty water causes skin and shell problems so get a powerful filter and clean the tank regularly. Terrapins need an ultraviolet light to stay healthy.

TAMING YOUR TERRAPIN

Terrapins are naturally shy, so you need to gain their trust. Start by feeding your pet by hand. Once it comes over when you approach, try picking it up. Always handle your terrapin gently and reward it with a treat afterwards. Wash your hands thoroughly after touching your pet.

BEST TERRAPINS FOR BEGINNERS

- Box turtles only grow up to about 15 cm (6 in) long, so they are easy to handle. They love to bask under a heat lamp in the early morning and late afternoon. Wild box turtles often hibernate in winter.

- Painted turtles need lots of swimming space and prefer not to be handled. They can live for more than 30 years and grow up to 25 cm (10 in) long. They hibernate in winter in the wild.

- Map turtles have attractive markings and grow up to 25 cm (10 in) long. They need good filtration and plenty of oxygen so it's worth adding an airstone to the water.

- Mud turtles spend more time on land than most other species. They rarely grow to more than 12 cm (5 in) long, but they're not hands-on pets. They can be grumpy and sometimes bite.

- Diamondback terrapins are active and inquisitive pets that grow up to 20 cm (8 in) long and need a large tank. In the wild, they live in brackish water, and stay healthier if a small amount of aquarium salt is added to their tank.

SALAMANDERS

Salamanders are nocturnal, but may adapt to being active during the day. Tiger and fire salamanders are most commonly kept as pets. They can live for more than 10 years and fire salamanders may reach 30 years old.

PICKING YOUR PET

Make sure you buy a salamander that has been bred in captivity. Choose an adult, because juveniles live underwater and need extra care. Fire and tiger salamanders can be kept in small groups in a large space, but males may fight over territory.

LIVING QUARTERS

Salamanders need a large, cool tank, with a thick layer of moist potting compost, coconut fibre or bark with hiding places, such as a flowerpot on its side. A shallow dish of chlorine-free water will keep the tank damp and give your pet somewhere to bathe. They need a temperature between 18 and 21°C (65-70°F), so a cool room is the best place to keep them.

UNDERSTAND YOUR PET

I like to burrow, so tap my tank to tell me when it's feeding time.

FEEDING

Salamanders like crickets, earthworms, wax worms and other bugs. Most prefer live food, but fire salamanders eat dead insects and chopped up worms. Feed adults two to three times a week and remove uneaten food after 20 minutes. Never leave live bugs in the tank – they may injure your pet's skin!

TANK MAINTENANCE

Salamanders produce a lot of waste, and bacteria soon builds up in damp conditions, so you should spot clean the tank every day and wash it thoroughly with warm water and a scrubbing brush every week. Rinse it with chlorine-free water afterwards. If mould appears in the tank, it is too damp.

HANDS OFF

Salamanders have delicate skin that can easily be injured. If you must pick up your pet, you should wash your hands in chlorine-free water and handle it with wet hands. Some species ooze toxic oil, so wash your hands immediately afterwards.

AXOLOTLS

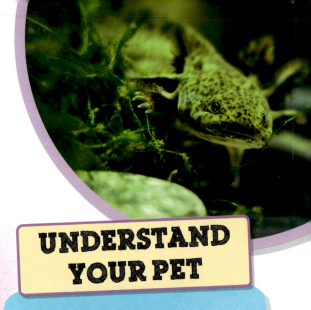

With their frilly gill stalks and wide grins, axolotls make charming pets. They are a type of salamander and are almost extinct in their native home, Mexico. Axolotls kept as pets are all bred in captivity.

SALAMANDERS THAT NEVER GROW UP

While most salamanders live in water as larvae, then take to the land, axolotls keep their cute larval features and spend their whole lives underwater. They live for 10-15 years and most reach 25 cm (10 in) long.

BOTTOM DWELLERS

Axolotls are active and live on the bottom of the tank, so need a long aquarium that holds at least 45 litres (10 gals) of water. They need a secure lid in case they try to climb out. Axolotls are loners, and may eat each other's limbs if they're kept together – they'll probably gobble up any other tank mates, too. Don't use gravel in the tank as axolotls may swallow it.

WATER QUALITY

Axolotl poop and waste food produces ammonia, so you need to grow friendly bacteria to get rid of it. A good water testing kit from an aquarium store will explain how. The water temperature should be 16-20°C (60-68°F). Treat tap water with chlorine remover – you'll need a filter with a weak flow. Clean the tank at least once a month, but don't remove all the water, or you'll lose your helpful bacteria.

To move your axolotl, catch it in a soft net made of fine mesh that won't damage its fingers and gills.

FEEDING YOUR AXOLOTL

Axolotls should be fed once a day on brine shrimp, bloodworms, earthworms or axolotl pellets. You can put the food in a bowl or a jar on its side, or feed your pet using tongs. Clear away uneaten food, otherwise it will rot.

KEEP IT DARK

Axolotls have weak eyes and hate bright light, so if you have a tank light, turn it off as often as possible and give your pet some dark hiding places such as a plant pot on its side, or some large aquarium ornaments.

NEWTS

Newts are active during the day and enjoy living in groups. They make interesting pets because they're always exploring, looking for food and interacting with tank mates.

WHAT IS A NEWT?

Newts are a type of salamander and Chinese and Japanese fire belly newts are the species most commonly kept as pets. They're semi-aquatic and like to spend time on land as well as in the water. They are happy at normal room temperatures and may live for more than 15 years.

A PERFECT HOME

You'll need a 45-litre (10-gal) tank for up to four newts, or double that for up to ten. A third of the tank should be dry. You can make a slope by gluing smooth rocks together with aquarium sealant and adding peat, sand or moss, or buy platforms from a pet store. Don't use gravel that's small enough for your pets to swallow, or anything with sharp edges.

UNDERSTAND YOUR PET

I'm an escape artist so make sure my tank has a well-fitting lid.

FEEDING

Newts enjoy bloodworms, crickets, earthworms and maggots, but they can live happily on pellet food if you don't want to handle creepy-crawlies. You should feed your pets every other day and give them as much food as they will finish in 15 minutes. Remove any uneaten live food after 20 minutes. Some newts will take food from their owner's hand.

KEEP THE WATER CLEAN

Newts need about 25 cm (10 in) of water at a temperature of 16.5-24°C (62-75°F) and it must be kept clean. If you have a filter you should change a quarter of the water every week, otherwise you'll need to change it every other day. A turkey baster is useful for this job because you can remove the dirtiest water from the bottom. Top it up with dechlorinated water or bottled spring water at room temperature.

HANDLING YOUR PETS

You should only handle your newt if it's absolutely necessary. Newts are very fragile and they secrete toxins from their skin that protect them from predators. If you must pick up your pet, wash your hands before and afterwards, or wear clean latex gloves.

FROGS

Pet frogs include terrestrial frogs that live on the ground, tree frogs, aquatic frogs that spend all of their lives in water and semi-aquatic frogs that live in water and on land.

WHO IS WHO?

A frog's name can sometimes be confusing – pixie frogs (called after their Latin name) grow into very large, fat African bullfrogs, for example, and Oriental fire-bellied toads are actually frogs.

Find out how large your pet will grow – some tiny pet-shop frogs grow into giants, and very large frogs don't move much so they can be quite boring (and long-lived) pets.

FEEDING YOUR FROG

Frogs eat a variety of live insects so if you're thinking of keeping frogs, you must be happy to handle these. Large frogs love mice pinkies, but they shouldn't have too many because they're quite fatty.

CHOOSING A FROG

- Fully-aquatic frog: African dwarf frogs are small and active. They spend their lives underwater, but they have lungs and breathe air from the surface, so they need a good amount of air space at the top of the tank. They do best when kept in groups, so get at least three.

- Semi-aquatic frog: Oriental fire-bellied toads are very active and are quite easy to care for, so they make good pets. They enjoy living in groups. Keep them in a tank with enough water so they can sit on the bottom with their eyes and nostrils above the surface. You can create a slope so they can leave the water, or float cork platforms on the surface.

- Tree frog: White's tree frogs are good pets for first-time frog keepers. They need a tall terrarium with a soil or bark substrate, and branches that they can climb. These frogs need a minimum temperature of 20°C (68°F) and humidity of 70-80%. They should be fed with live bugs two or three times a week.

- Terrestrial frog: Pacman frogs – named after the video game – get quite large, but they aren't very active so a 45-litre (10-gal) tank is large enough for them. They need a substrate that they can burrow into, such as coconut fibre or moss and a shallow water bowl that they can sit in. They are nocturnal and should have a temperature no lower than 18°C (65°F).

UNDERSTAND YOUR PET

I like a change of scenery, so rearrange the branches in my tank to keep me entertained.

MADAGASCAR HISSING COCKROACH

'Hissers' are one of the largest cockroach species. They come from the island of Madagascar off the African coast, where they often live in fallen logs. Unlike most cockroaches, they don't have wings.

GENTLE GIANTS

Madagascar hissing cockroaches grow up to 7.5 cm (3 in) long and live for two to three years. They are easy and cheap to keep and have a gentle nature. They hiss as a warning when they are disturbed and males hiss to attract a mate. Although cockroaches are associated with dirty places, hissers are very clean creatures and don't smell.

HISSER HOME COMFORTS

A 45-litre (10-gal) tank is big enough for several hissers. Make sure it has a very tightly fitting lid, because cockroaches can walk up glass and will soon escape if there are any gaps. Your hissers will need somewhere to hide from the light so add some cardboard tubes or egg cartons, or for a more natural look, get a bark tunnel.

HOT AND HUMID

Giant cockroaches come from the tropical rainforest, so they are happiest at temperatures of 24-32°C (75-90°F). Spread damp coconut fibre or potting compost over the base of their tank and keep the enclosure moist at all times by spraying it with water. Cockroach tanks don't get very dirty, but they should be cleaned regularly because moulds can grow that cause allergies in humans.

FOOD AND DRINK

Hissing cockroaches enjoy fresh fruits and vegetables, especially carrot, apple and banana, and they need high protein food too, such as dry dog or cat food. Remove any leftover food so it doesn't go mouldy. Give your pets a little dish of water with a piece of sponge or cotton wool in it to stop them drowning. They will also suck water droplets from the side of the cage when you spray it.

BREEDING

It's easy to tell the difference between male and female hissers as males have horns at the back of their head. Unless you have homes for large numbers of baby cockroaches you should get two males. Hissing cockroaches give birth to live young and if you have a mixed-sex pair, or your female pet has been in contact with a male, you could end up with 20 to 60 babies.

STICK INSECTS AND MANTISES

Stick insects and praying mantises have different diets, but they both need similar homes. A tank, vivarium or even a large, tall sweet jar will be suitable for either pet. You should spray their enclosure with water every few days so they can drink droplets off the leaves.

A TALL ENCLOSURE

Stick insects and mantises shed their exoskeletons by clinging to a branch and stepping out of the old one. They need an enclosure that's at least three times as tall as a fully grown adult insect. If they don't have space to slide out of their old skeleton, they may get stuck and die. The floor should be covered with kitchen towel for easy cleaning and the top should have ventilation holes, or be covered with netting, so your pets have fresh air.

A LEAFY DIET

Stick insects need fresh foliage at all times. Place branches in a jar of water. These leaves are suitable: privet, rose, oak, hazel, bramble (older leaves only, not the pale green new growth). Make sure they haven't been sprayed with insecticide or weed killer.

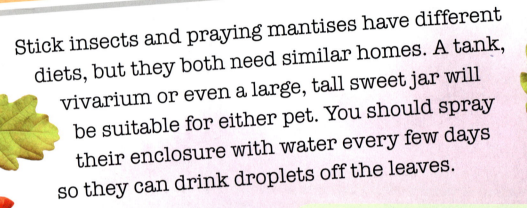

BREEDING

Females can produce young without a mate. If you see eggs at the bottom of the enclosure it's best to remove them, or you'll have a stick insect population explosion.

PRAYING MANTIS ENCLOSURE

Praying mantises like to perch up high, so fill their enclosure with branches or artificial plants that they can climb on. The base should be covered in a material that can be kept damp, such as kitchen towel, potting compost, shredded bark or sand, so the enclosure stays humid. Mantises come from warm parts of the world, so your pet may need a small heat pad in winter.

AN INSECT DIET

Mantises are ambush predators – they lie in wait ready to pounce on their insect prey. If you're not happy feeding them live insects, a praying mantis isn't for you. An adult mantis will eat one or two crickets or flies a day, and uneaten prey should be removed after an hour.

MOULTING

A mantis will stop eating a day or two before it sheds its exoskeleton. It's especially important to remove uneaten food from the enclosure at this time because a freshly moulted mantis could be injured by its prey. Don't feed your mantis for 24 hours following its moult and never try to pick it up during this time.

UNDERSTAND YOUR PET

I grow wings when I'm an adult, so I might fly away if you let me out.

GIANT LAND SNAILS

Snails don't need a tall tank, but they need lots of room to move. Some people keep them in a clear under-bed storage box with ventilation holes in the lid. Snails like to burrow, so fill it with at least 5 cm (2 in) of sterilised soil and add pieces of bark for your pets to hide beneath. The soil should be moist, but not wet, and the temperature should be 20-25°C (68-77°F). You'll need a tightly fitting lid to stop your pets escaping.

FEEDING

Giant African land snails need a constant supply of fresh fruit and vegetables. They love apple and banana, but their main food should be leafy greens and cucumber. Always remove uneaten food so it doesn't rot. Snails need calcium to keep their shells strong, so keep a piece of cuttlefish bone in their enclosure.

BREEDING

Snails are hermaphrodites, which means that they are both male and female, but you still need two snails to produce young. In the right conditions, they make nests of round white eggs. If you want more snails, remove them gently and put them in a container of damp potting compost. They will hatch in about two weeks. Snails produce large numbers of eggs, so you should dispose of them if you don't want more pets.

HEALTH TIPS

Giant land snails may carry salmonella, so always wash your hands after handling your pets or cleaning their enclosure. If the conditions in the tank are not right, your snails may seal up the opening to their shell. In this case, check that the temperature and humidity are right and try to get them to open up by bathing them.

EVERYDAY CARE

Snails need a bath about once a week to keep them clean and free of pests. Put them in a shallow bowl and gently pour water over their shell and body. Don't cover their breathing hole or they will drown. If their shells are especially dirty, you can clean them with a soft toothbrush but never use soap. Tanks should be cleaned about once a month and you should change the soil every week.

UNDERSTAND YOUR PET

Never pull me off the side of the tank by my shell as it could come off!

UNUSUAL PETS QUIZ

How much do you know about your unusual pet pals? Take this quiz to find out.

1 What sort of animals are chinchillas and degus?

a. Reptiles
b. Rodents
c. Amphibians

2 How do you know if a chinchilla is too hot?

a. It starts to sweat
b. It lies on its back
c. Its ears go red

3 When are degus most active?

a. During the day
b. At dawn and dusk
c. At night

4 How long should a snake's tank be?

a. A third of its adult length
b. Its full adult length
c. Twice its adult length

5 Why are axolotls different from most salamanders?

a. They spend their whole lives on land
b. They are vegetarians
c. They spend their whole lives underwater

6 Why should you avoid handling your newts if possible?

   a. They have very fragile skin
   b. Their skin produces toxins
   c. Both of these

10 Which of these is a giant land snail's favourite food?

   a. Banana
   b. Dried dog food
   c. Crickets

7 What sort of amphibian is an Oriental fire-bellied toad?

   a. A terrestrial toad
   b. A semi-aquatic frog
   c. A tree frog

8 How do you tell male and female hissing cockroaches apart?

   a. Males have wings
   b. Females are lighter in colour
   c. Males have large horns at the back of their head

9 Why do stick insects and praying mantises need a tall enclosure?

   a. They need a lot of exercise
   b. So they have room to step out of their old exoskeleton
   c. So they have room to jump

QUIZ ANSWERS

1 What sort of animals are chinchillas and degus?

b. Rodents

2 How do you know if a chinchilla is too hot?

c. Its ears go red

3 When are degus most active?

a. During the day

4 How long should a snake's tank be?

b. Its full adult length

5 Why are axolotls different from most salamanders?

c. They spend their whole lives underwater

6 Why should you avoid handling your newts if possible?

c. Both of these

7 What sort of amphibian is an Oriental fire-bellied toad?

b. A semi-aquatic frog

8 How do you tell male and female hissing cockroaches apart?

c. Males have large horns at the back of their head

9 Why do stick insects and praying mantises need a tall enclosure?

b. So they have room to step out of their old exoskeleton

10 Which of these is a giant land snail's favourite food?

a. Banana

GLOSSARY

airstone – A piece of equipment that increases water circulation and the amount of oxygen in the water.

ammonia – A stong smelling chemical that is harmful to animals.

amphibian – Cold-blooded animals that start life underwater as larvae with gills. As adults, most grow lungs, breathe air and live on land.

aquatic – Living in water.

bacteria – Microscopic living things that are found everywhere. Some are dangerous and cause diseases, while others are helpful and keep animals healthy.

brackish – Slightly salty water, found where seawater and river water mix.

chlorine – A chemical in tap water that kills bacteria.

cold-blooded – Animals whose body temperature changes according to their surroundings.

dechlorinated – Remove chlorine from water by using a chemical or leaving it to stand overnight.

diabetes – A disease that leads to too much sugar in the blood.

exoskeleton – An outer shell that supports and protects an insect's body.

foliage – Plant leaves.

gills – Organs on the side of the head that act like lungs and absorb oxygen from water.

hibernate – To sleep during winter.

humidity – The amount of moisture in the air.

invertebrate – An animal without a backbone.

juvenile – A young animal.

larvae/larval – Newly-hatched form of a fish, amphibian or insect.

neutered – An animal that has had an operation to stop it having babies.

nocturnal – An animal that sleeps during the day and is active at night.

parasite – An animal that lives in or on another creature and feeds from it (often by sucking its blood).

Mice pinkies – frozen or live baby mice that do not yet have fur.

predator – An animal that hunts and eats other creatures.

salmonella – Bacteria that cause stomach upsets.

secrete – To produce and ooze.

semi-aquatic – Living both on land and in water.

shedding – To lose skin or hair.

substrate – The material (often earth, gravel or sand) on the floor of a tank.

terrarium – A glass-fronted tank for small land animals.

terrestrial – An animal that lives on the ground.

toxic/toxins – Poisonous/a poison or venom.

ultraviolet (UV) light – Light that makes up about 10% of sunlight and is divided into UVA, UVB and UVC. Humans cannot see UV light but some animals can.

INDEX

A
Airstone – 13
Amphibians – 5
Aquarium – 13, 16, 17, 18
Axolotls – 5 16-17

B
Babies – 5, 23
Baby mice – 10
Bacteria – 15, 16
Bathing – 15, 27
Bloodworms – 17, 19
Breed – 5, 23, 24, 26

C
Cages – 4, 6, 7, 9, 23
Cardboard – 7, 9, 23
Chewing – 4, 7
Chinchillas – 4, 6-7
Crickets – 15, 19, 25

D
Damp – 5, 9, 15, 23, 25, 26
Degus – 4, 8-9
Diseases – 5
Dust bath 6, 7, 8

E
Earthworms – 15, 17, 19
Eggs – 5 24, 26
Exoskeleton – 5, 24, 25

F
Food – 7, 9, 10, 12, 15, 16, 17, 18, 19, 23, 25, 26
Frogs – 20-21
Fur – 6, 7, 8

G
Giant land snail – 26-27
Gnawing – 4, 9
Gravel – 16, 18

H
Handling – 4, 5, 10, 12, 13, 15, 19, 20, 27
Hay – 6, 7, 9
Heat lamp – 4, 10, 12, 13
Hibernations – 13
Hiding places – 23, 26

I
Insects / bugs – 5, 12, 15, 20, 21, 24-25
Invertebrates – 5

L
Lifespan – 5, 6, 8, 10, 11, 12, 13, 14, 16, 18, 20, 22

M
Madagascan hissing cockroach – 22-23
Mould – 15, 23
Moulting – 5, 25

N
Nest – 6, 9, 26
Neutered – 6
Newts – 5, 18-19
Nocturnal – 6, 11, 14, 21

P
Pellet food – 7, 9, 12, 17, 19
Poop – 16
Praying mantis – 25

R
Reptile – 4, 10
Rocks – 11, 16
Rodents – 4, 10

S
Salamander – 5, 14-15, 16, 18
Salmonella – 4, 27
Scent – 6
Shedding – 5, 11
Shell – 5, 12, 26, 27
Snails – 5, 12, 26-27
Snakes – 4, 10-11
Stick insects – 24
Swimming – 12, 13

T
Taming – 7, 10
Tank – 10, 12, 13, 15, 16, 17, 18, 19, 21, 23, 24, 26, 27
Temperature – 4, 6, 9, 15, 16, 18, 19, 21, 23, 26, 27
Terrapins / turtles – 4, 12-13
Toxic – 15, 19

U
Ultraviolet light – 4, 9, 10, 12

V
Vegetables – 9, 12, 23, 26
Vivarium – 10, 24

W
Water – 5, 7, 10, 11, 12, 13, 15, 16, 18, 19, 20, 21, 23, 24, 27
Wild – 5, 13